YOUR PATH AHEAD

by

Jeff Smith

Your Path Ahead
Don't Dig A Student Debt Hole Your Career Can't Fill
Jeff Smith

Visit our website at www.yourpathahead.com.

ISBN-10:   0989677605
ISBN-13:   978-0989677608

Printed by Createspace

Book Design by Nick Papadis
Illustrations by John Welter
Editing by Julie Mathis

First Edition: (8/2013)

Disclaimer: This publication is designed to provide accurate and personal experience information in regard to the subject matter covered. It is sold with the understanding that the author, contributors, publisher are not engaged in rendering counseling or other professional services. If counseling advice or other expert assistance is required, the services of a competent professional should be sought.

Table of Contents

Chapter 1

The Path of the US and the World

Two students are walking down a path when they encounter a bear. The first student bends down, takes his running shoes from his backpack, and puts the shoes on. The second student says, "Are you crazy? That won't help you outrun the bear."

The first student replies, "I don't have to outrun the bear – I just have to outrun you."

The world is competitive. Grades. Sports. Careers. Hard work results in an increase in your quality of life. Start with the end in mind, set goals, and develop

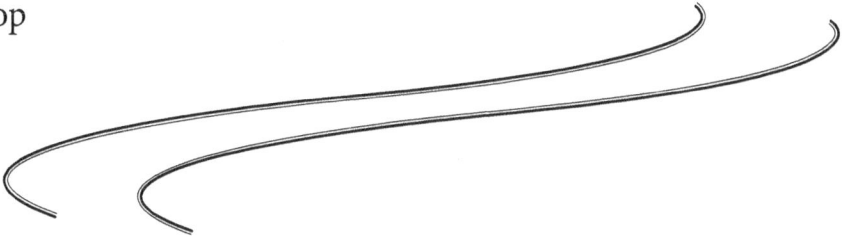

Your Path Ahead.

World Population

Throughout history, the world experienced "normal" population growth, where population decreased by age. There were always more newborns than one year olds, more 5 year olds than 10s, and more 20s than 30s – and the same throughout all age ranges. Life expectancy was shorter. Simple infections that are now easily treated often resulted in death.

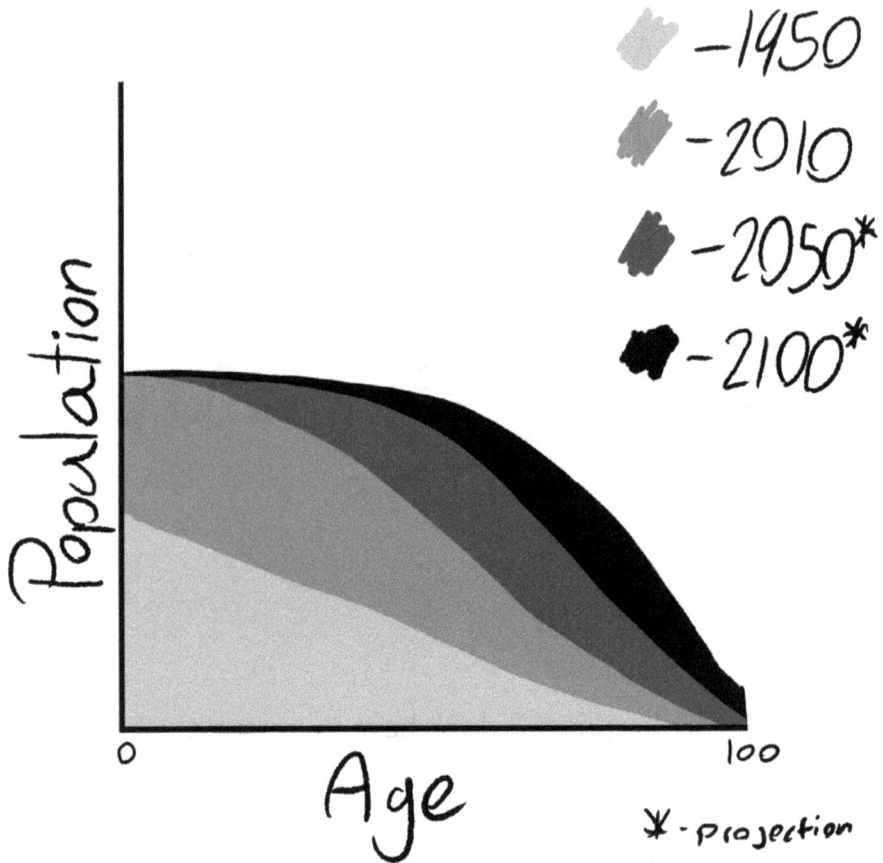

Now that negatively sloped line is flattening, from a combination of two factors:

- Better health and healthcare
- Slowing of the birthrate
  o   Birth control
  o   People marrying and starting families later in life

Projections for the future show a continued "widening" at the top ranges. Humans will continue to expand in lifespan, living longer. While total population will continue to grow, the age components (average age) will continually shift older.

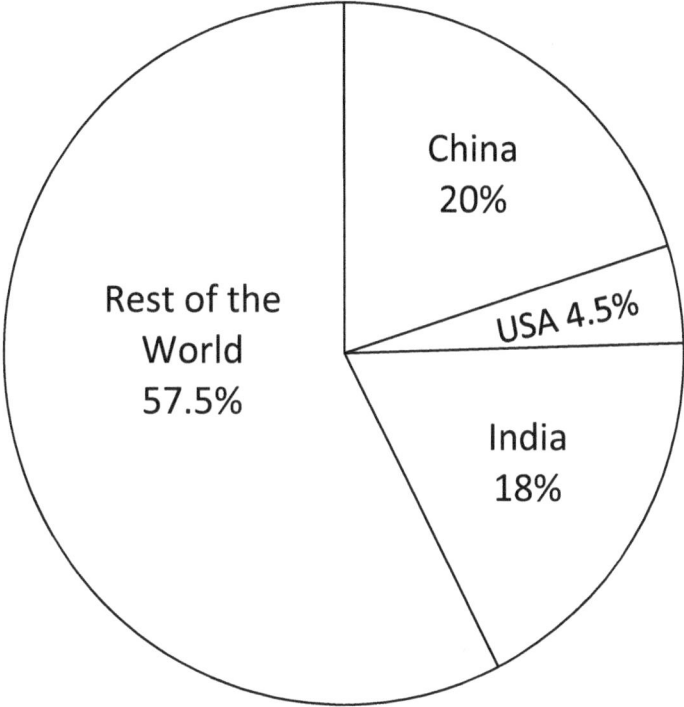

China
20%

Rest of the
World
57.5%

USA 4.5%

India
18%

Nearly 40% of everyone on this planet lives in two countries – China and India, yet those two countries comprise only 1% of the number of countries on earth. Less than one out of every 20 people in the world live in the United States, yet the US is the world's largest economy. China will replace the US as the world's largest economy by the end of this decade.

Japan is among the world's most rapidly aging countries. In 1950, there were nearly 10 Japanese citizens under age 20 for every person over age 65. The forecast for the year 2025 is that there will be two Japanese people over age 65 for every one under age 20.

The chart below shows the median age of the population of Japan and the expected change over your lifetime. Median means that half of the population is older, and half of the population is younger than the median age.

Japan

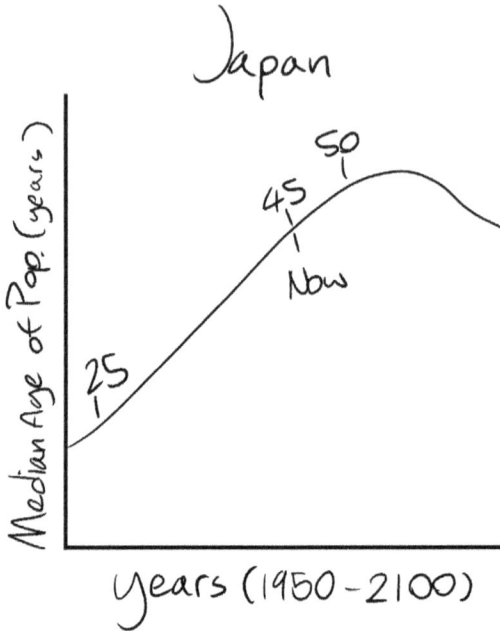

While not as extreme as Japan, the United States is also expected to have a significant increase in the median age of the population in your lifetime.

United States

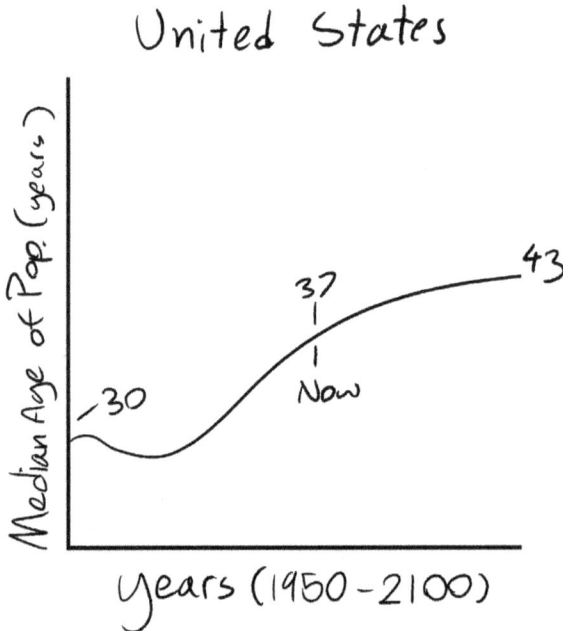

The old-age dependency ratio is the ratio of the population aged 65 years or over to the population aged 20-64. Currently there are ten people age 20-64 for every 2 people 65 and over. This ratio will be close to ten to four in 20 years, and the charts shows that in your lifetime there may be only two people age 20-64 for every person 65 and older. This ageing of society will apply the most significant financial pressure on the United States government, and also on everyone working and paying taxes.

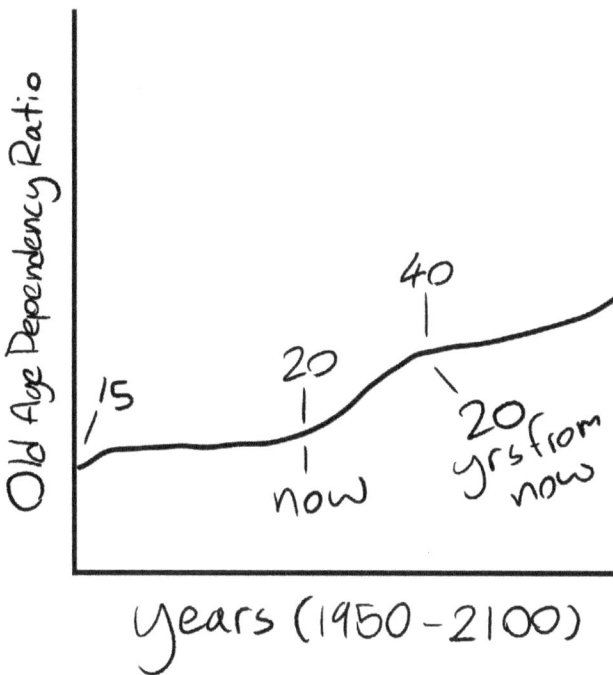

The **Information Age** or technological revolution – is defined by the advancement, assimilation and availability of knowledge. Information is the raw material that the workforce of the future will utilize and transform into their final work product.

Since the end of World War II, the United States has been the economic power of the world, where other countries have had to rebuild from the damages and effects of the war. For the majority of the time since then, it has been relatively easy for the United States to advance economically resulting in a higher standard of living.

In relation to the rest of the world, the United States is a relatively young society. All the natural resources necessary to advance society existed across America, creating opportunities to fulfill The Great American Dream. Sometimes, however, it is easier to start new than to change existing culture. The United States has always attracted those from foreign lands who possessed initiative and the desire for lifestyles that could be realized here. The US has remained an economic powerhouse by utilizing the resources that have been available.

	Reading	Math	Science
1	China: Shanghai	China: Shanghai	China: Shanghai
2	Korea	Singapore	Finland
3	Finland	Hong Kong	Hong Kong
4	Hong Kong	Korea	Singapore
5	Singapore	Chinese Taipei	Japan
17	USA		
23			USA
31		USA	

The chart above suggests that the United States has been living off the stockpiles of components that position us as the leader in the world economy, while other countries have worked harder and focused on education as the springboard to future economic growth. For decades after WWII the United States was the leader in all educational measures. Now the United States has dropped to the 31st position in math, 17th in reading, and 23rd in science.

Education Attainment

↓

Productivity

↓

Economic Growth

↓

Higher Per Capita Income

↓

Well Being/ Better Lifestyle

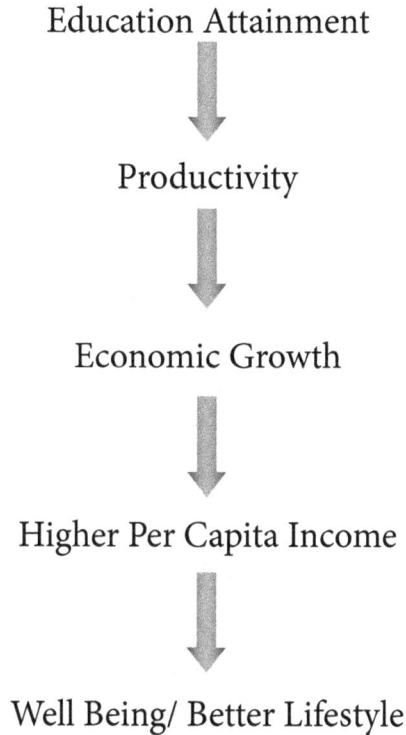

This is one of the two most important issues that will affect all generations in the future, but primarily the Flip Generation (see page 29). The economies of other countries will grow and advance faster than the economy of the United States. This will translate into better jobs and higher incomes that result in better lifestyles.

Education is available, accessible and can be an exceptional value only if you make it a priority in your path to happiness and desired lifestyle. **Start with the end in mind.**

People are **good** at what they **like**, and **like** what they are **good** at doing. Everyone has different talents and skills. Some we are born with, others we develop. People are different in size and physical abilities. The **KEY** to developing your Path and Goals is matching your skills, talents and abilities to general and specific areas of focus that match your talents and skills.

Integrate what you are good at and enjoy with your plans for the future.

Don't look for advice – look for guidance.

One day Alice came to a fork in the road and saw a Cheshire cat in a tree. "Which road do I take?" she asked. "Where do you want to go?" was his response. "I don't know," Alice answered. "Then," said the cat, "it doesn't matter."

*from Alice's Adventures in Wonderland by Lewis Carroll

Educational Attainment

In general, the age of 18 has been considered the threshold of reaching adulthood for 100 years. Before that, it was 14 with most people having to start work at that age.

The chart below indicates that in 1940 approximately 25% of the United States population (25 years old and older) had attained a high school degree. It was the late 1960s before half of our population had attained high school educations.

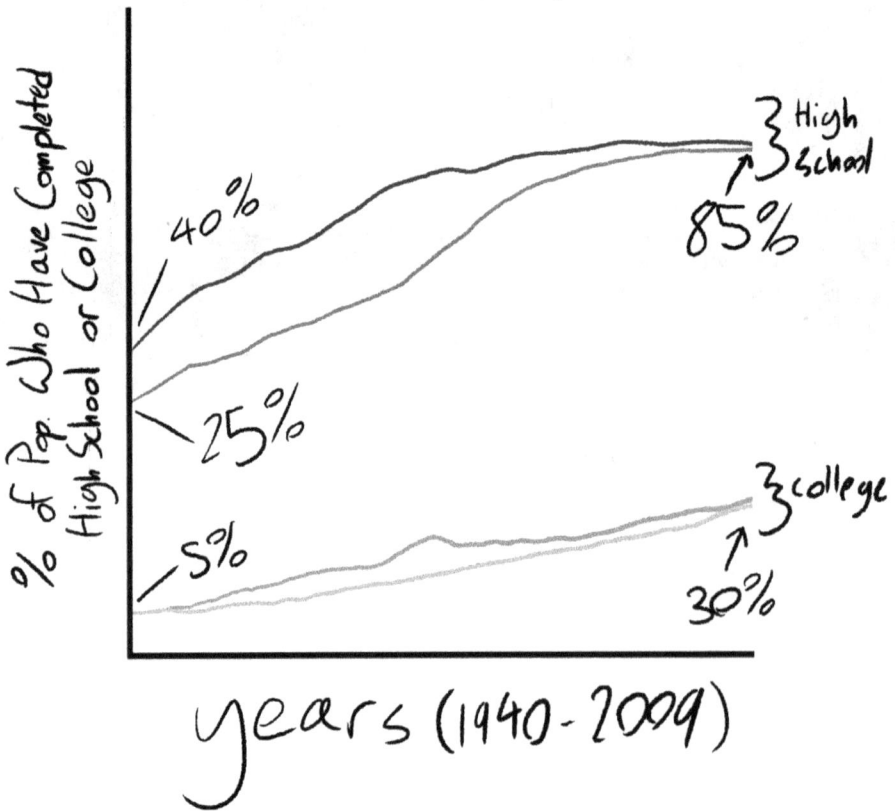

● - 25-29 yrs, High School +   ● - 25-29 yrs, Bachelor's +
● - 25+ yrs, High School +   ● - 25+ yrs, Bachelor's +

% of Pop. Who Have Completed High School or College

40%

25%

5%

} High School

85%

} college

30%

years (1940-2009)

In 1940, around 5% of the population had a college degree, which means 20% of those that had finished high school, had also graduated from college. Now, less than 30% of our nation's population over age 25 has attained a college degree.

To remain competitive in the world economy, the United States must increase the skill level of its workforce. Fifty percent of students entering college drop out before completing their degrees. Most of these students drop out because they did not start with a plan, or goal, in mind.

Current research indicates the brain develops until the age of 25. Surveys of adults reveal that most Americans consider the age of 26 the benchmark for becoming an adult.

In reality, most individuals grow up either when they have to, or when they want to.

Individuals change more in their twenties than in any other stage of life. It is your twenties that clearly define your path in life. The choices you make today determine your options tomorrow. **Do your future self a favor; think about your future and create options.**

Federal Deficit

A deficit is when more money is spent (expenditures) than comes in (revenues) in a year. The national debt is the total of the deficits, for all years. Spending more than the money coming in is known as deficit spending.

It is similar to an individual making $40,000/year and spending $62,500. The difference, $22,500, must be borrowed. An individual can only continue to spend more than they earn for a short period, because banks and credit card companies will stop lending them money. The United States cannot continue this deficit spending that adds to our national debt. Here is how the debt translates to individuals:

Deficit	$4,200	Per American
	$9,200	Per Working American
Debt	$54,000	Per American
	$120,000	Per Working American

Less than half of Americans work, and projections for the future indicate the percentage of non-working Americans will steadily increase. Future workers will be responsible for repaying this national debt that resulted from deficit spending.

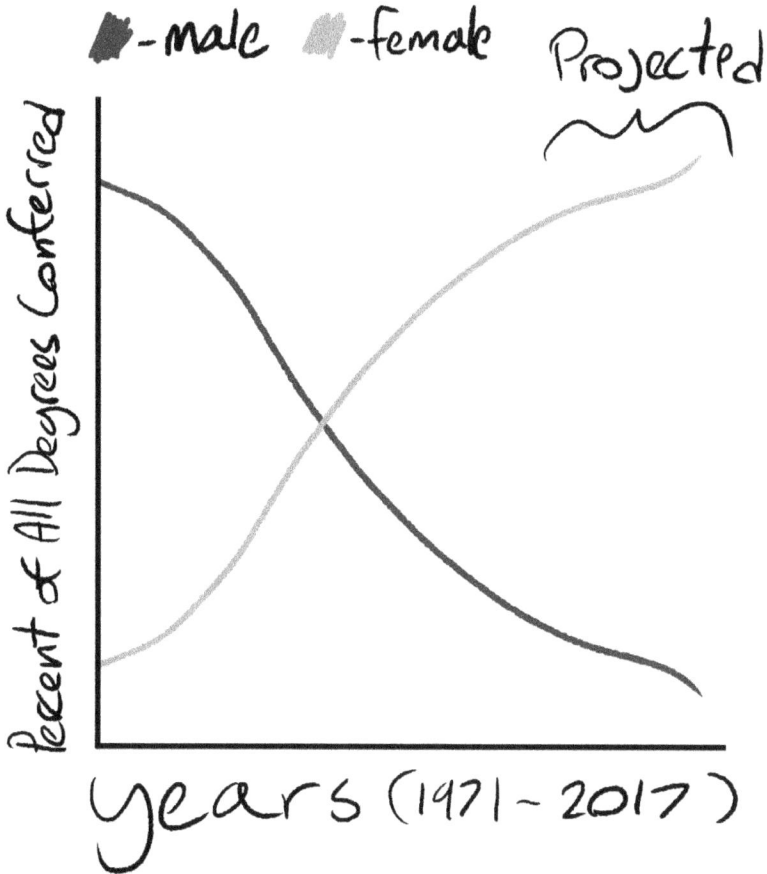

■ - male ■ - female   Projected

Percent of All Degrees Conferred

years (1971 - 2017)

Male vs. Female Graduation Rates

Women passed males in number of college graduates annually in the early 1980s. Now more than 6 women graduate from college for every 4 men. Women passed men in post-graduate degrees (masters, doctorates, and professional degrees) in the late 2000s. If these trends continue, the workplace and the workforce of the future will shift demographically, resulting in a society where women are the primary earners and also the majority of the professionals and managers.

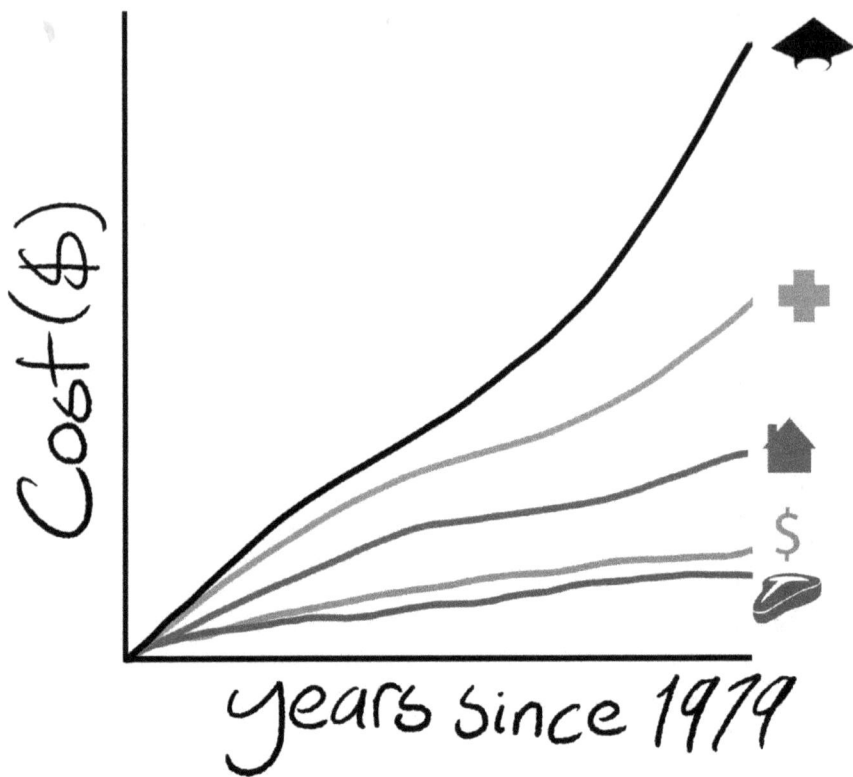

Since 1979

		1979	Now
Tuition		$1,000	$11,500
Health Care		$1,000	$6,000
Shelter/Housing		$1,000	$3,300
Average Prices (CPI)		$1,000	$2,600
Food		$1,000	$2,350

Explosion in Tuition

The growth in college tuition has risen at a rate of nearly 5 times the rate of food, energy and consumer prices. There are many causes, and likely the most significant is the availability of student loans. Loans allow colleges and universities to continue raising tuition, requiring students to shoulder the added expense by acquiring more student loans. Total student loan balances have passed $1 trillion, and the average college graduate has over $27,000 in student loans.

State support, per student, has also declined significantly during this period as more students pursue post-secondary education. This is in part because state revenues and availability of funding to support education has declined.

These issues dominate the national news and these trends will correct over time. For anyone pursuing post-secondary education, the issue is not why it costs so much or how to fix it, but how to navigate the current system and continue on your path to accomplishing career and life goals **without digging a student debt hole your career can't fill.**

Hey Man, I Need a Plan

A student walked into a professor's office and said "Hey, man." The professor replied "Hey, man." This continued on for a moment – man, yeah man, man, man, etc. until the student finally stated: "Hey man, I need a plan."

The student was in need of a plan of study as required to qualify for federal student loans because his grades had dropped below minimum standards. Colleges and universities often encourage students to continue to enroll in classes while on probationary status and borrow additional funds if necessary, in efforts to increase enrollment and maximize revenues. Colleges and universities in the US are largely tuition driven models – most of the financial support to schools for operations comes from student tuition.

The professor did his job, as required by the university, and advised the student in the courses necessary for the degree. This professor also asked the student what his goals were. Did he have a definitive direction? Why was he in school? The student replied, "Man, everybody just tells me I need to be in school."

"Man," as the professor refers to the student, enrolled for another year, borrowing an additional $23,000 for college expenses. He flunked out of college that year, and the experience left him with a total of 28 college credit hours and $53,000 in student loans. Without a college degree, he has a student loan payment of $610 monthly for the next 10 years, unless he prolongs the terms to 15 years to get the payment down to $470 for the longer period.

Summary of The Path of the US and the World

- Your generation will have to compete for the better jobs and careers

- US and world population will flatten, which will inhibit economic growth

- The choices you make today determine your options tomorrow

- Retirees will continually increase in percentage of the population, applying more financial pressure on the working population to provide for the older generation's wellbeing

- China will India comprise 40% of the world's population

- The drop in educational attainment in the United States will allow other countries to advance at a faster pace than the United States

- The United States cannot continue to borrow money to pay bills, and the money borrowed must be paid back

- Women have passed men in earning post-secondary (after high school) degrees, and this will significantly affect the workplace of the future

- Start with the end in mind

- Do what you like and are good at doing

- College costs too much. That won't change soon.

- Don't dig a student debt hole your career can't fill

Chapter 2

The Path of Time

Rate of Change

Rate of change is the speed at which a variable changes over time. The following charts indicate the rate of change of all the factors that measure the advancements that improved the wellbeing of humans – the amount of change between generations and over lifetimes.

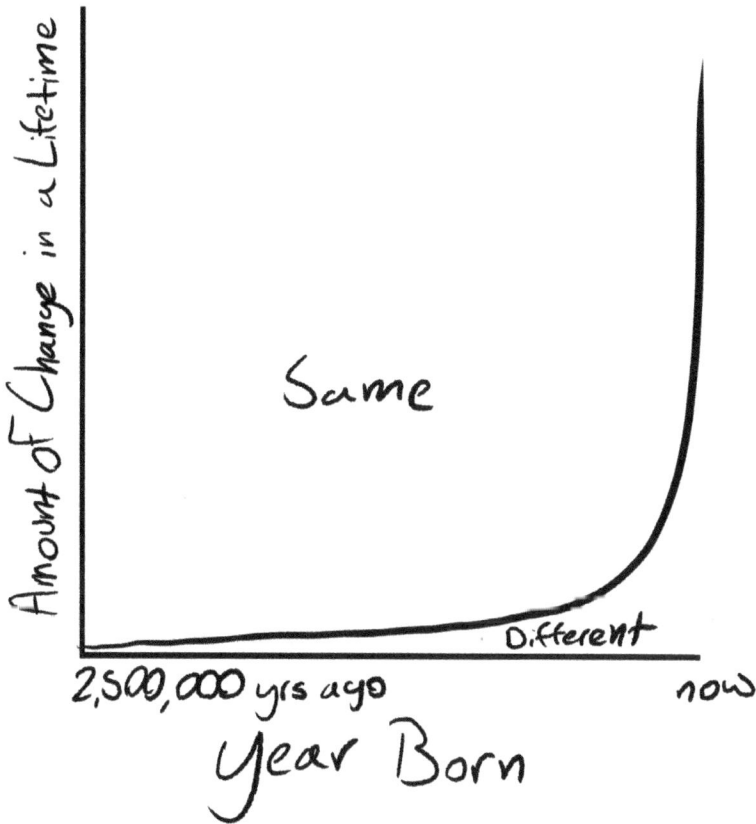

For millions of years, the change in how people lived their lives from generation to generation was barely measurable. If you had been born more than 25 generations ago, you would have lived your life nearly identically to that of your parents and grandparents. As you see in the graph above, more things stayed the same than were different. The line does have a slight, but gradual slope up, because over time life did change very, very slowly.

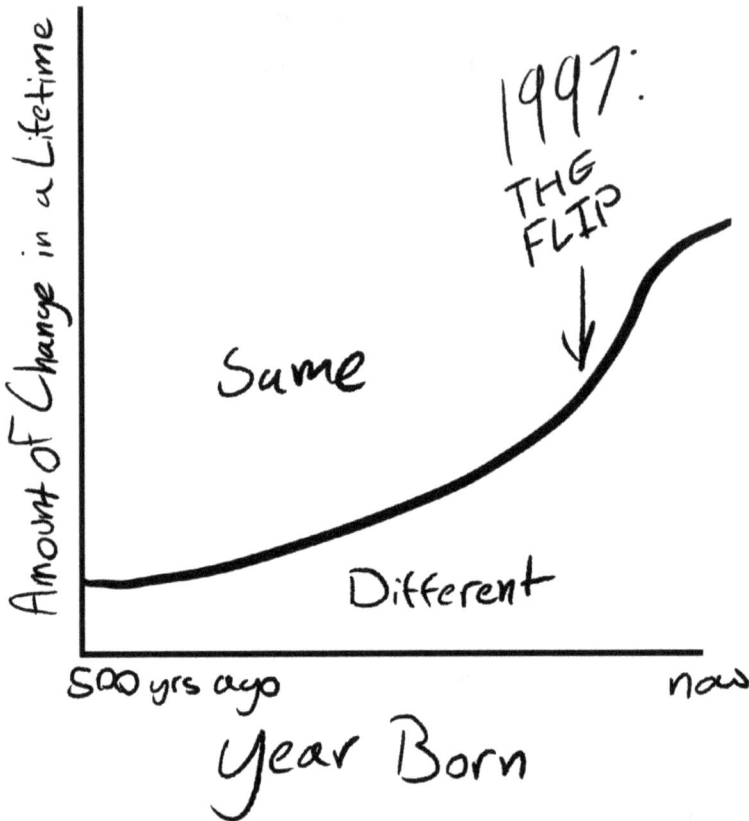

The Dark Ages lasted nearly ten centuries. In the 1400's the printing press was invented, which made owning books possible for the average person, and knowledge and information became available to society. Knowledge and information gave birth to the Renaissance, which began the first significant increase in the scope of the Rate of Change line. The Industrial Revolution continued to increase the rate of change, as productivity increased more than 10 times because of the efficiencies and technology of methods of mass production. There were significant advancements in the late 1800s in the United States – railroads, the automobile, steel mills, electricity and the financial system. World War II changed society significantly socially. Men went to war, and women filled their vacant jobs, often in factories producing military goods. After the war, many women stayed in the workforce, deciding they liked their own paychecks and the financial independence.

Today females comprise 50% of the workplace, a dynamic that has changed drastically over the last 100 years. Generation X and Y came from families where significant numbers of mothers worked, where in previous generations the vast majority of mothers were at home.

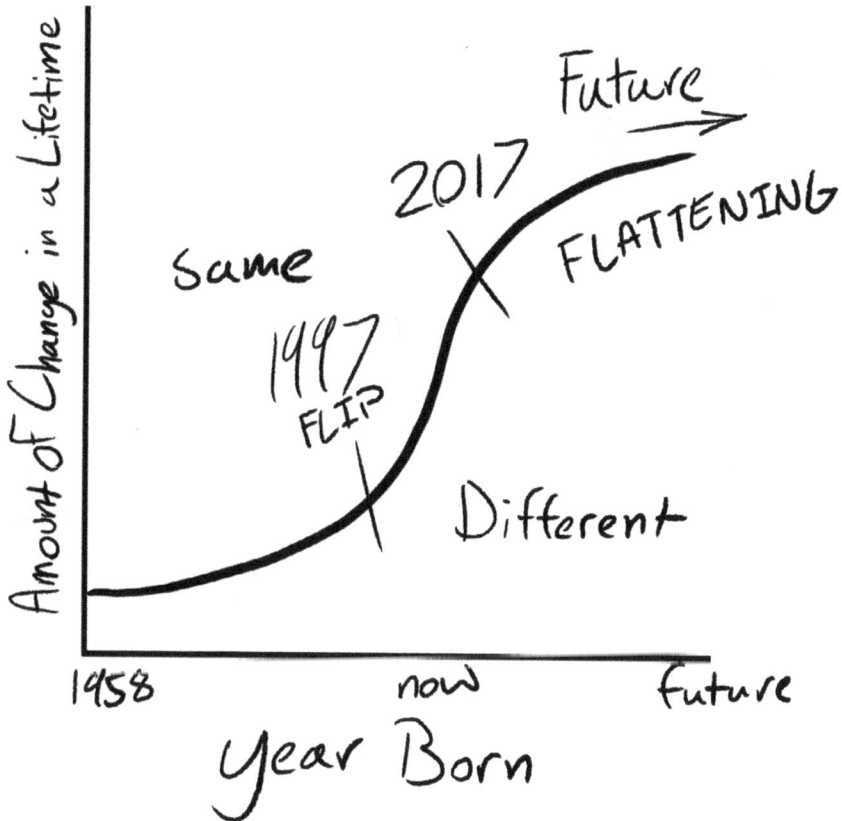

Around 1997, the rate of change "flipped," meaning more became different than was the same, due to rapid advancements in technology – therefore it is the beginning year of the "Flip Generation." The rate of change continues this steep climb until approximately 2017, when it begins to slow. Change will still be occurring – just not as fast. Smartphones, for example, will continue to change and do more, but in perspective, that change is not nearly as significantly as the change from land lines to cell phones to smart phones, in a relatively short time.

Timeline of Change

Stone Technology (scrapers)

125,000 Generations ago

1st stage of advancement in life – Thought

First use of leverage and first indication of cognitive thought that separates man from other species

Hand Axe

80,000 Generations ago

First known **Innovation** - Thought progresses as man developes a tool.

Fire

75,000 Generations ago

For warmth and cooking – indicated mankind leveraging and innovating from materials available in their environment

Timeline of Change (cont.)

Shelter

25,000 Generations ago

Increased probability of survival while satisfying increased need for comfort.

Clothes

8,500 Generations ago

Increased mobility, as previously man selected location based on two requirements – food supply and warmth

Tools

5,000 Generations ago

Creative thought- both in making tools and the objects made using tools.

Flute

1,750 Generations ago

Indicates more to life than survival

Ceramics

1,200 Generations ago

Another example of how you live life gaining importance over basic survival

Domestication of Animals

750 Generations ago

Leveraging of energy, harnessing of power – using animals to do the work

Plow & Agriculture

500 Generations ago

Began the **2nd stage of advancement in life –**
Agricultural – and the birth of **Civilization**. By growing food, man became stabilized in location, villages were created, interaction and cooperation expanded, and trade (first commerce) developed

Wheel

300 Generations ago

Significant advancement in respect to productivity and leveraging available energy

Gnomon (sundial)

275 Generations ago

Substantial advancement in thought – utilization of time and application of perspective of time. Developments in mathematics and written communication as planets were charted and calendars initiated

Pyramids

230 Generations ago

Proof of major progression in the capabilities of the mind

Timeline of Change (cont.)

Sail

130 Generations ago

Leveraging the power of the wind to significantly increase productive capabilities

yoink

Crane

125 Generations ago

Leveraged energy to hoist materials for building. Replaced ramps - greatly increasing efficiency.

Waterwheel

115 Generations ago

Captured the energy available in moving water. Even today a main issue with power is the storage of energy, required to match available energy with the time energy is demanded for use.

Books

100 Generations ago

Stabilization of communication, increased storage of knowledge, and improved consistency in written communication

Chess, Backgammon, & Toilet Paper

75 generations ago

Furtherance of the civilized lifestyle. Advancements in productivity increased time available for leisure activity, and established use of thought (games for the mind) as pleasurable

Printing Press

29 Generations ago

After the Dark Ages (the thousand years of darkness in knowledge and economic regression), this momentous development made **knowledge available** to the average person and provided the tools that led to the Age of Discovery.

Renaissance & Age of Discovery

25 Generations ago
Leonardo Da Vinci and the advancement of art, architecture, literature, and learning.

Newspaper

20 Generations ago
Increased availability and timeliness of information

Industrial Revolution

12 Generations ago
3rd stage of advancement in life – Industrial. The most significant advancement in quality of life in history. Over 150 years, per capita income increased 8 to 10 times. Productivity, trade, and availability of goods are all identifiers.

Telegraph

9 Generations ago

The most disruptive and significant advancement in communication in history was the telegraph. The Pony Express reduced the time to send messages from St. Louis to California by 10 days. Eighteen months later, the telegraph began to send messages back and forth across the same area with a tap-tap-tap, resulting in the end of the Pony Express.

Electric Light

6 Generations ago

Manufacturers had largely been restricted by daylight, and the electric light allowed the addition of shifts, resulting in huge increases in productivity and efficiency by utilizing the same space, tools and machines all day and night, if needed. There were many additional social and personal aspects, as people could utilize daylight for outdoor activities and rely on power and light at night for dinner, reading, etc.

Automobile

6 Generations ago
Instant personal mobility, which expanded nationalization.

Airplane

6 Generations ago
Mobility expanded to the world – globalization.

Radio

5 Generations ago
Instantaneous availability of information and entertainment.

Television

3 Generations ago
Added depth to the significant impacts of radio – a picture is worth a thousand words.

Transistor

3 Generations ago
4th stage of advancement in life – Information. The birth of technology.

PC

2 Generations ago
Knowledge stored and available for processing personally, and virtually everywhere.

Internet

Availability of information – everything, everywhere and always

The Future- Probabilities and Possibilities

- The Cloud – access information anywhere you are connected
- Everything works – efficiency, productivity
- Smartphones – central to all communications
- Automated manufacturing – less jobs making, more jobs designing
- Big brother sees all – less privacy
- Always connected - everywhere
- Robots as caregivers for the elderly – aging society
- Using noise and vibrations to recharge devices – harnessing energy from ambient sounds
- Pocket Doctors – devices that know you're starting to get sick before you do
- Decline of the corporation – don't expect to work at one place all your life
- Space age – travel and scientific advancement
- The brain – understanding why we are who we are
- "Learning" will replace "Education" – learn to learn
- The moon is the earth's battery – stored solar energy on the moon will power the earth
- United States goes cashless, eventually the world – multiple devices will act as debit cards
- "Changing" clothes takes new meaning – fabrics that change color, and can adjust size
- "Sustainability" – know and understand, it will apply to everything
- Earth will run out of oil – replaced by solar, wind, wave, fuel cells, geothermal, artificial photosynthesis, traveling wave reactors and more
- Increased urbanization will increase global warming
- Water must be managed wisely – will cost more than gas if not managed
- Under the sea – people will live there, grow food, harness energy

- "Made on the Moon" – Manufacturing on the moon will be a reality. One example is to build satellites more efficiently than on earth
- Housing, buildings advance – collect and store energy, convert waste into energy, recycle food waste to grow new foods
- Most people will live past 100 – medical advancements and knowledge of healthy lifestyle
- More bicycles – health, convenience
- Eliminating the annoyance of insects – healthier, scientific methods to control mosquitoes, insects that destroy crops, etc.
- Non-journalist journalists – Experts in fields will write about what they know instead of journalists attempting to write what they don't know. Writing and communication skills will be necessary to combine with other skills
- More and more jobs "outsourced" – Companies, organizations and institutions will employ managers who will pay by the job to get tasks done.
- Non-developed areas will develop – Deceleration of urbanization will increase the migration of people and enterprises to areas such as Canada, the Artic regions, Iceland, and Russia which have vast amounts of undeveloped territory.
- The world will eventually become non-territorial – trade, efficiencies in governance, inter-marriage and relationships. These changes will be gradual but constant.
- Consistent shift in transportation to mass and public avenues – one example is car sharing, using small efficient cars when only personal transport is needed, then using vehicle with more storage when needed.
- Technology will virtually eliminate wars – Anyone wanting to start a fight can be identified and technologically isolated.
- The "Social Matrix" – Social interaction utilizing technology will change the basic structures of education and work. Both will become more collaborative within groups.
- Individualized medicine – individual genetic analysis to produce individualized treatment

- Obesity trends will be reversed – Exercise, diet, and the availability for both will be a focus.
- Continuing change in religion – Religious structure will continue to evolve, yet remain a personal choice.
- Less demand on building and expanding roads – mostly technological advancements in coordinating traffic flows, as well as slowing of population growth and changes in work traffic (fewer 8:00 to 5:00 jobs)
- More automation leads to more unemployment – Unskilled labor is on the path to elimination.
- "Middle" skills will lead the way – carpenters, plumbers, electricians, medical assistants
- Changes in economic power – The United States, with less than 5% of the world population, will be surpassed by China this decade as the leading economy – but the growth in China will slow as they face issues with education, food, energy, water etc.

Generations

Generations are defined by the events and the environment that surround them at birth, and then by their generation's affects on society.

Generations	Born between	Shaped by
Lost	1875 1900	World War I
Greatest	1901 1924	World War II
Silent	1925 1945	The Depression
Baby Boom	1946 1963	Redefined Traditional Values
Generation X	1963 1979	The 60s
Generation Y	1980 1996	Divorce and the Corporation
Flip	1997 2016	Change and Technology
Flat	2017 2035	Deceleration of Change
Singularity	2036 →	Learning Systems (systems that teach themselves)

Agriculture/Manufacturing/Service/Information

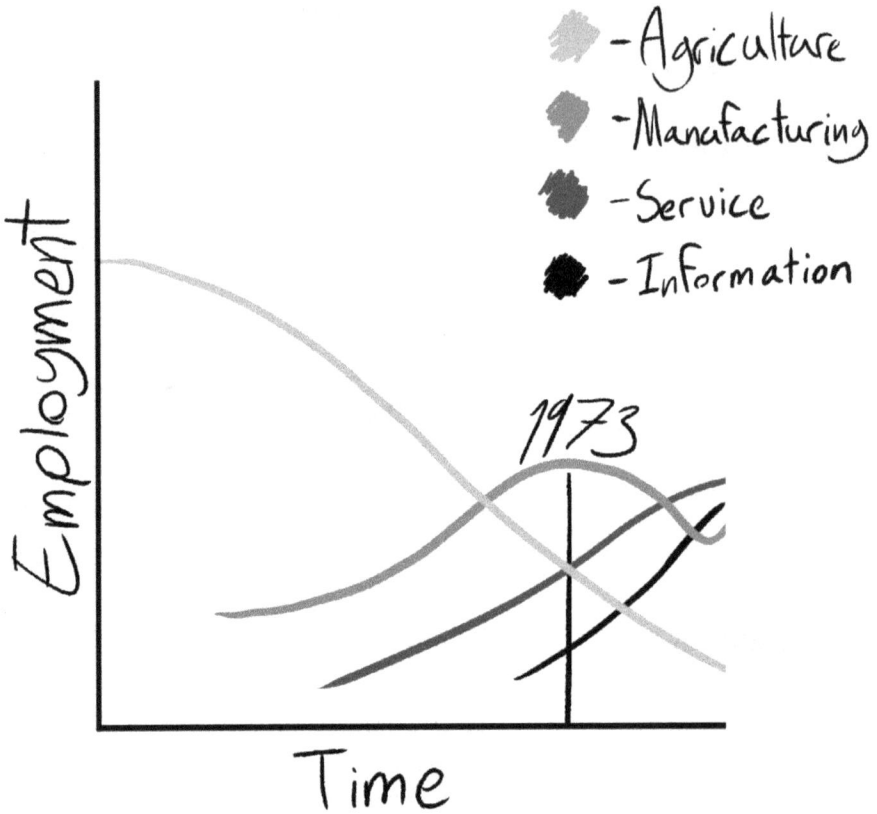

The chart above shows the percentage of the population's employment by sector over time. It can also be viewed as exhibiting the effects of increasing productivity over time. For most of the history of mankind, life was about survival, and food was the primary necessity. Hundreds of years ago the majority of jobs involved growing and producing food. Advancements in technology in **agriculture** (machinery, fertilizers and chemicals, bioengineering) reduced the percentage of the population whose primary function or employment was in agriculture. Currently, less than 2% of the US population is employed in the agriculture sector. In the 50 year period from 1950 to 2000, productive measures resulted in one farmer in the year 2000 being able to produce the same output as 12 farmers in 1950.

Manufacturing replaced agriculture as the primary driver of the economy and economic wellbeing. Manufacturing employment peaked somewhere around 1973 in the United States and began its decline primarily from foreign competition, where lower labor costs in countries like China made it more effective to manufacture in China and ship to the United States. Now several factors (foreign labor costs rising and increased productivity from technological advancements) are allowing the US to regain a competitive advantage in many markets – resulting in a rise in manufacturing.

The **service** segment is dominated by skilled labor (low, middle and highly skilled) and professions. Examples of middle skill professions are sales, construction, machinists, welders, production workers and installation/repair jobs like auto mechanic and heating and air conditioning technicians. Highly skilled jobs include computer science, engineering, financial analysis pharmacy, law, and medicine. Severe shortages of skilled labor (middle and high) are projected for the future in the United States as the baby boomers retire and there is not enough qualified skilled labor available to replace the retirees.

The Flip Generation is defined by change and the availability of **information**. Search engines and the internet turn any device into a world library. Methods of processing and presentation of information will consistently change and increase in efficiencies. To be successful in this segment workers must be fluid (able to change) and have developed strong skills in accessing, analyzing and synthesizing information, critical thinking, communication, problem solving and creativity.

Change Between Two Generations

Don, Frank and Bill graduate from different colleges in 1950. They all have a liberal arts degree, which at the time was the most prevalent. The three young men were all hired by the same manufacturing company and entered into their management training program. The first month Don worked first shift, Frank the second shift, and Bill the third shift. The next month they alternated and continued to do this throughout the 6 month training program. Don left the company after 10 years, Frank worked there for 25, and Bill worked there 44 years, working his way to president before retiring.

Their grandchildren graduate from college over 60 years later. Don's granddaughter, Sydney, majors in math and completes her master's degree in applied mathematics. The job market is strong for her skills, and she has her choice of jobs and locations to live. Don's grandson, Palmer, focused all his energy and applied himself in the field of chemistry. After his master's completion, he worked for several years applying his knowledge. He, too, had many options for jobs and areas to live. After several years of work, he knew his passion was research and returned to school to pursue a PhD.

Frank's grandson, Nelson, finished with a degree in history as he was undecided what he wanted to do. He bounced around from job to job, and while he mostly remained employed, he is what is considered "underemployed" because many of his jobs, like bartending, don't require a college education. Frank's granddaughter, Leigh, is a dancer. She teaches dance lessons, and has been in multiple musicals and plays. She loves her life, and continues to follow her passion.

Bill's grandchildren have taken varied paths in their life and career choices. One is an attorney. Another is a teacher. A third is a plumber. The fourth grandchild has not found his path in life and has always been unable to support himself.

The world has changed rapidly between these two family generations. When Don, Frank and Bill entered the workforce, employers were looking for "well rounded" individuals. Institutions and industries hired the best available individuals and trained them for the specific requirements they needed. Many people from the Greatest Generation and those that preceded it stayed at one job their whole career.

Entering the job market now is the opposite from two generations ago. Companies no longer have the luxury of training employees for months. Employers hire candidates that possess the specific skills necessary to be productive the first day at work.

The United States Department of Labor predicts that the individuals from the Flip Generation will have an average of 10 to 14 jobs – BEFORE they reach age 38. Currently 1 of every 4 workers have been at their jobs less than 1 year, and half of all employed have been at their jobs less than 5 years.

Summary of The Path of Time and Change

- Change that affected quality of life has been slow throughout history but now the rate of change has peaked

- The Flip Generation is the first generation where more is different than the same

- Technological advances cannot continue at the same rate, and the rate of change will slow

- The Timeline of Change shows the advances that significantly affected the way people lived their lives

- Knowledge of future trends will allow you to think about potential careers and set goals and make plans

- The time periods in which people are born are labeled "generations," and the generations are shaped by the events and environments at their birth and then by how they contribute to society

- Life was about survival; food, shelter, and warmth. As humans progressed, technology increased productivity in agriculture, leading to a shift from farm jobs to manufacturing factories. Advances made manufacturing more efficient, shifting the labor market to the service industry. Now the growth in jobs will be in the information (knowledge) segment.

- Companies used to train people, and people remained at the same jobs for long periods. Now companies want to hire people who already have the skills necessary for the job, and people now switch jobs often.

Chapter 3

The Path of Wellbeing and Happiness

Goals

Develop your 5 year goals. Once you have set these objectives, you can then develop your plan to achieve these goals.

- Review and adjust or update your goals every year. You can do this on our website at yourpathahead.com
- Goals should be attainable – setting goals too high (unattainable) is the recipe for failure
- Rank goals in order of priority
- 5 goals – can be more or less, but keep near 5

Laura is a junior in high school. Here are Laura's goals:

1. Attain college degree in Education with certification in Elementary Education
2. Finish degree remaining under Your Path Ahead's Maximum Student Debt Guideline for the degree
3. Improve fitness
4. Travel to a foreign land
5. Explore musical interests (sing in a play, sing for a band, write songs)

With her goals established, Laura then developed her plan to achieve her goals.

- Graduate from high school, taking AP classes or dual enrollment that will be accepted toward her college degree
- Investigate and visit colleges that offer accredited degrees
- Develop financial plan for college to remain under Maximum Student Debt Guideline
- Develop fitness plan, workout structure and schedule
- Read and search internet about foreign lands and rank by interest
- Use "free" time for musical interests

Skills to Develop

1. Critical thinking, problem solving, decision making, questioning

2. Accessing, analyzing and synthesizing information

3. Communication – written and oral

4. Innovation, Curiosity, Creativity, Imagination

5. Agility, Adaptability, Flexibility

- These skills MUST be integrated into EVERY learning platform.
- Always be THINKING how to apply EVERYTHING you learn

While in school, integrate the skills above into all the content of your courses. Think about what you can do with the information and the knowledge you are gaining to open future paths of opportunity.

Learn how to use information instead of memorizing. Learn how and where to find the information needed to make informed decisions.

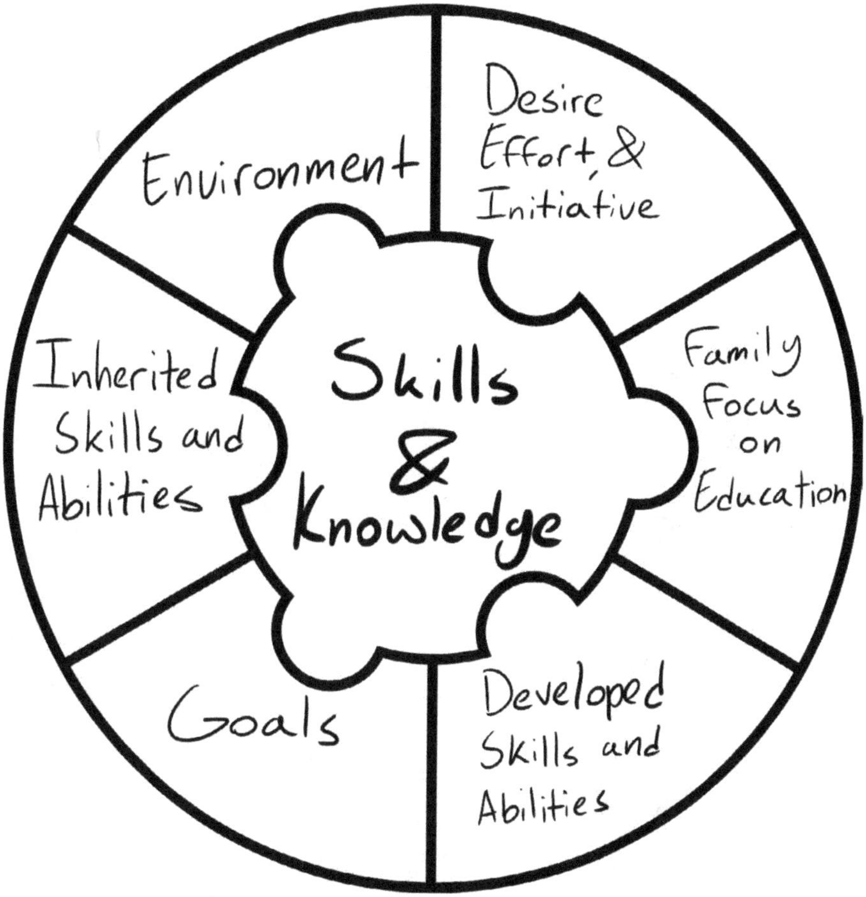
Environment
Desire
Effort, &
Initiative
Family
Focus
on
Education
Developed
Skills and
Abilities
Goals
Inherited
Skills and
Abilities
Skills
&
Knowledge

- **Learn to learn.** It will be the most important skill you can develop for life

- You connect the puzzle pieces that direct Your Path Ahead

- Investigate and explore jobs and careers that match your strengths

Mankind has used thought and our increasing ability to think to become more productive, which has constantly led to increasing the quality of our lives. Physical labor has transitioned to mental labor. To be prepared for financial independence you must focus your efforts on increasing your skills and abilities to create **options** in Your Path Ahead.

Critical Thinking and Problem Solving

Employers are increasing pre-employment testing to assure that the individuals hired possess the desired skills and knowledge needed to position their organizations successfully in the growing knowledge economy. Besides basic math and language skills, employers are assessing critical thinking abilities – accessing, analyzing and synthesizing information and the ability to solve problems and make decisions.

Below are 12 questions, similar to those you could see on a pre-employment test in the future. Answers can be found on page 105. For detailed solutions, go to our website - yourpathahead.com

1. What if you are selling cell phone cases for $5 and you know that every time you raise the price $.50 you sell 5% less cases. Can you calculate at what sales price per case you maximize sales revenues?

2. Add this information – your cost for the cell phone cases is $2 each. Can you calculate at what sales price per case you maximize your gross profit?

3. Amanda, Katie and Melissa start a business together and agree to split the profits equally. Amanda invests $60,000, Katie invests $52,500, and Melissa invests $37,500. If profits are $28,800, how much less does Amanda receive than if the profits were divided in proportion to the amount invested?

4. Your friend places 4 cards - an Ace, King, Queen and Jack - face down but not necessarily in that order. You have one chance at guessing what the cards are in order. You friend tells you that you guessed n cards correctly. Which value of n (0,1,2,3,4) is not a possible value of n?

5. It takes Mike and Bruce two hours to build a wall. It takes Mike and Warren 3 hours to do the same job, and it takes Bruce and Warren 4 hours to do the same job. How long would it take Mike, Bruce and Warren to build a wall if all 3 men worked together?

6. Claire and Becky begin walking on a circular track at the same time. Claire finishes each lap in 6 minutes, and Becky finishes each lap in 10 minutes. How long will it take Claire to be exactly one lap ahead of Becky?

7. Levon is 18 years old and his cousin Suzanne is twice as old. When Levon is 25 years old, what will be the age of his cousin?

8. Iggy's power bill for November was $90. In December, it increased by $15. In January it increased again, this time by $30 from the previous month. What was Iggy's average power bill for these three months?

9. The Austin family went to Europe for the summer vacation. It rained for exactly seven days while they were on their trip. On the days it rained, it rained either in the morning, or the afternoon, but not both. There were exactly five afternoons it did not rain, and six mornings it did not rain. What is the length, in days, of their trip?

10. Sydney stayed up late studying, woke up late, and was in a hurry to get to class. When she walked along the path to her school, Sydney met the Chipmunk and the Duck resting under a tree. The Chipmunk lies on Mondays, Tuesdays and Wednesdays and tells the truth on the other days of the week. The Duck, on the other hand, lies on Thursdays, Fridays, and Saturdays, but tells the truth on the other days of the week. They made the following statements:

Chipmunk: "Yesterday was one of my lying days."

Duck: "Yesterday was one of my lying days."

From these two statements, Sydney was able to deduce the day of the week. What day was it?

11. The professor took a cup filled with water and drank 1/5 of its contents. When the professor looked away, the student refilled the cup by adding alcohol to the remaining water and then stirred. The professor drank 1/4 of this liquid mixture. When the professor looked away again, the student refilled the cup with more alcohol and stirred. The professor drank 1/3 of this liquid mixture. When the professor looked away a third time, the student refilled the cup with more alcohol. What percent of this final mixture was alcohol?

12. How many total squares are in the picture?

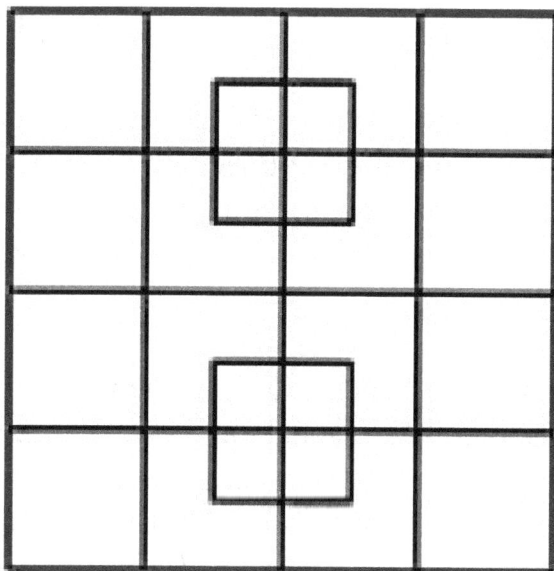

Back to the Same Job

Jed quits his job at the Quickie Quackie, a convenience store, to return to learn at Local U. He is 27 and only has a few credit hours from previous attempts at college work when he was younger.

It is October of his last semester, and he goes out after class with other students for a few beers. The discussion evolves to student loans. Jed states that he has student loans. The conversation continues, with each student discussing their various levels of debt and payment options. Jed stays out of the discussion because he does not know his balance. When the discussion turns to employment, Jed states his desire to return to Quickie Quackie as a store manager.

The next day he goes to the financial aid office at Local U and gets his balance of $58,500. The financial aid counselor informs him that the actual balance is higher because a portion of his loans are unsubsidized – meaning interest accrues while still in school and is added to the balance. His balance at graduation is $61,800.

When Jed quit work at Quickie Quackie he was earning $22,000/year. After graduation he is hired as a manager at Quickie Quackie at a salary of $31,000/year. His new salary is $9,000/year greater than his old one, which results in an additional $525 of take home pay monthly. However, Jed's student loan payment is $711 per month. Although he has acquired a higher paying position, his monthly take home pay is $186 lower than when he previously worked at Quickie Quackie before he returned for his degree.

Start with the end in mind.

Summary of The Path of Wellbeing and Happiness

- Set 5 year goals

- Develop a plan to achieve goals

- Develop skills

- Advancements over time have reduced the amount of physical labor

- In the future, labor (work, jobs) will be more mental

- Being able to think and solve problems will be the key to successful careers

- Understand the return before borrowing money for college

Chapter 4

Your Path Options

Spending

One third of the average American household's money goes to housing, one fifth to transportation and one eighth for food. Insurance, savings, taxes, clothes, entertainment, health care, educational expenses, and all other living expenses total the remaining one third.

If you exceed our maximum recommended student loan debt per degree (on page 75), you must choose where you will take the reduction. Generally reductions are taken in housing, which explains why the number of graduates moving home with parents after graduation has more than doubled in the last eight years. Graduates are staying with parents because salaries are not going up, and the average payback period on student loans is 15 years.

Where will your money go?*

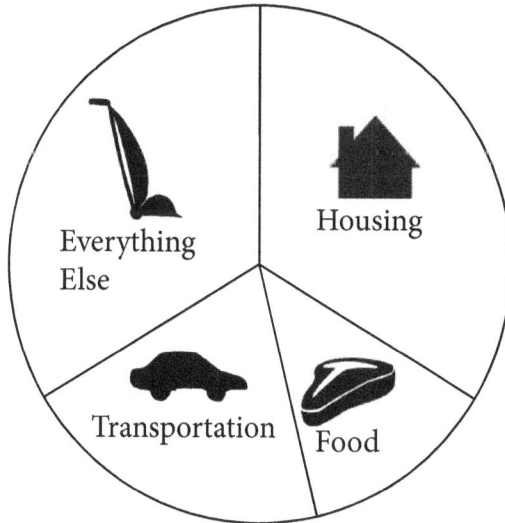

*Net paycheck after taxes and other withholdings

Typical Work Day

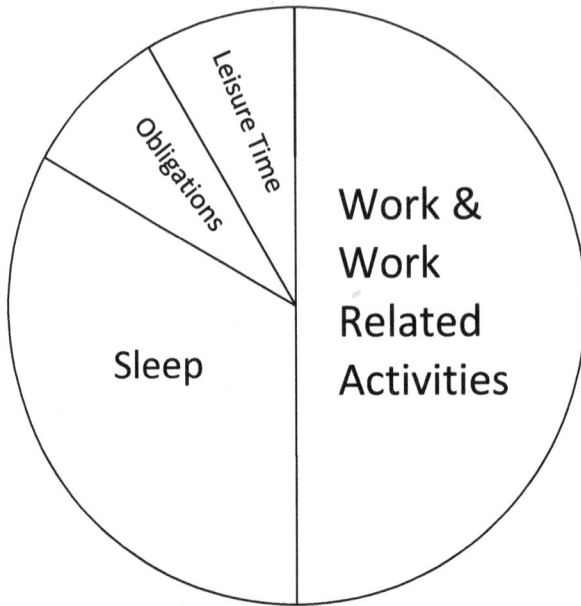

Your generation can expect to work for 50 years. Approximately half of your work day will be captured by work and work related activities – such as commuting and preparing for work. One third of the day is reserved for sleep, leaving on average, 4 hours a day for obligations and leisure activities.

People spend a third of their lives working, and a third sleeping. Think about how you want to spend your life and develop goals that align to the lifestyle you desire.

Double Half

When you go to work, your output must double your input, or your input will be half your output.

Output – Your productivity at work

Input - $ in your pocket

Ex:	Salary	$50,000
	Deductions/Withholdings (30%)	- $15,000

	Take Home Pay	$35,000

*If you are making $50,000, your take home is $35,000.

But...

Your output is more than $50,000.

Your employer is responsible for employee taxes, insurance, etc. (benefits) This is usually 30% above your salary.

Ex:		
	Salary	$50,000
	Insurance, Taxes, Etc. (30% Benefits)	+$15,000

	Total Cost to Employer	$65,000

*It costs your employer $65,000 to pay you a salary of $50,000.

Now...

You will NOT be employed just to assist the company to breakeven. You must add value. In other words, you must cost the company less than what you make it.

Ex:

Salary ($50,000 x 10% Profit)	$5,000
Total Cost to Employer	+ $65,000

	$70,000

*You must generate at least $70,000 in output (productivity) to realize $35,000 of input (take home pay).

Happiness Equation

Happiness may be defined as an individual's level of well-being and contentment. To calculate, list the most important components of life, and PRIORITIZE, listing your most important component in life first, etc. Happiness is a function of the various elements of life over time, such as money, jobs, health, living location, possessions, emotions, and relationships.

	Chuck		Matt		Buck
1	Love	1	Career	1	Partying
2	Friends	2	Money	2	Romance
3	Family	3	House	3	Games
4	Career	4	Car	4	Food
5	Money	5	Hunting	5	Money
6	Location	6	Romance	6	Sleeping
7	Pets	7	Sports	7	Laughing
8	Faith	8	Learning	8	Working out
9	Running	9	Reading	9	Hobbies
10	Movies	10	Cooking	10	Traveling

Chuck's Happiness Equation indicates more focus on friends and family than on career and financial reward.

Matt is more focused on financial achievement and material possessions and is willing to lessen the emphasis on other components.

Buck seems focused on having fun at the expense of the responsibilities of life.

The Outcome of the Happiness Equation:

Choose how you want to live your life by developing your own Happiness Equation and then preparing for the career/jobs that will allow that lifestyle by acquiring the skills necessary for that career/job. You will find that life is a "zero sum game." You will have options that require choosing between alternatives. An example of this is being offered a promotion and pay raise that requires you to move 1,000 miles. Here you must choose between a path of financial gain and furthering your career over location and possibly proximity to friends and family.

Take the Path

Go to our website at yourpathahead.com to Take the Path. Travel along the path and answer the questions that are presented at each stage. At the end you will be able to view the possible meanings of your answers. This tool is designed to assist you in defining what is important to you in life, and align your desired lifestyle to education and career goals.

Would You Marry Someone With a $1,070/month Student Loan Payment?

Annie goes to a traditional four year public university out of state – a five hour drive from her home. She borrows the money for tuition, books, and room and board. She attends this institution for two and a half years before deciding to transfer to public university near home. She is working as a waitress while attending school. Annie loses credit hours when she transfers, and loses additional credit hours when she changes her major to sociology. She continues to borrow for school and finishes her degree in five and a half years. Her student loan payment of $1,070 per month (for 10 years) began the month after she graduated.

Annie meets Ben and they end up dating. Ben also started at a different school and lost credit hours when he transferred. Ben worked and saved his money for a few years and returned to college to pursue a degree in marketing. Ben owes $23,000 in student loans and his goal is to finish his degree without acquiring any additional debt. He graduates with a $265 monthly payment.

Kate also attended the same college as Ben and attained her degree in sociology. Kate wanted to start her path for her career without any student debt. She attended the local community college her first two years and completed the general education requirements required by Local University. She lost no credit hours by transferring. She graduates with no student loan payment.

Degree: Sociology

Kate & Annie

Yearly Salary	$36,100
Monthly Salary	$3,008
Take home pay (monthly)	$2,106

Annie

Student loan balance	$93,000
Student loan payment	$1,070
Available after loan payment	$1,036

Available to Spend After Graduation	Kate (No Loans)	Annie (With Loans)
Housing	$702	$345
Transportation	$421	$207
Food	$281	$138
Everything Else	$702	$345
Student loan payment	$0	$1,070
Total	$2,106	$2,106

Degree: Marketing

Available to Spend After Graduation	Ben (With Loans)
Housing	$654
Transportation	$393
Food	$262
Everything Else	$654
Student loan payment	$265
Total	$2,228

Ben

Yearly Salary	$38,200
Monthly Salary	$3,183
Take Home Pay (Monthly)	$2,228
Student Loan Balance	$23,000
Student Loan Payment	$265
Available after loan Payment	$1,963

Annie is forced to move back home because her student loans prevent her from being able to both rent an apartment and buy a car.

Your life, and the paths you choose, are paved by your decisions. Because the rate of change (more different than same) crossed-over for the Flip Generation, your decisions will be different and require more planning, than for your parent's and grandparent's generations.

Ben has a unique decision. He recognizes that should he marry Annie, she brings a $1,070 per month student loan payment to the marriage. This severely affects their lifestyle and their ability to purchase a home and start a family.

Annie has dug a hole that will greatly restrict her lifestyle for at least 10 years. In hindsight, she realizes she made two big mistakes:
1. Choosing an out of state public university just because she wanted to "get away from home." Out of state tuition is usually two or three times the rate of in-state tuition.
2. She had no plan of expected outcomes when she began college.

Ben stayed within Your Path Ahead's Maximum Student Debt Guideline for his selected degree. His student debt is manageable and he has positioned himself to explore options in his career and life.

Kate sacrificed some of the "college experience" in order to attain her degree debt free. Now she has maximized her ability to pursue the career and lifestyle she desires.

No other generation has been faced with these decisions which are the result of the explosion in tuition and student debt. Annie could have prevented digging a student loan debt her career can't fill by understanding that money borrowed for school should stay below Your Path Ahead's Maximum Student Loan Guideline.

* Studen Loan payment based on the prevailing interest rate of 6.8% for a 10 year loan term.

Summary of Your Path Options

- Two thirds of your money will go to housing, transportation and food

- One third of your money will be left for everything else

- Exceeding Your Path Ahead's maximum debt per degree guidelines will most likely prevent you from pursuing the lifestyle you choose

- Work and work related activities take 75% of the hours you are awake on a typical work day – a significant change from being in school

- The average college student spends 30 hours a week in class and studying

- The Double Half explains that you must produce twice what you "bring home" in salary

- Define your own Happiness Equation and integrate this into career decisions

- Look at all your options before exceeding the Maximum Student Debt Guidelines

  - o In state public colleges and universities
  - o Private colleges that significantly discount tuition to be competitive with public institutions
  - o Community colleges
  - o AP/CLEP
  - o Scholarships
  - o Living at home during college

- Start with the end in mind

Chapter 5

Your Financial Path

Maximum Student Debt

The average student takes 15 years to pay off student loans.

- The number of graduates aged 29 to 34 buying a house for the first time has dropped in half the last 10 years.
- 85% of college students move back home after graduation.
- 15% of graduates ages 25 – 34 live with their parents.
- More than 1 in 7 delay marriage because of debt.
- 1 in 5 delay having children.

Your Path Ahead recommends maximum dollar amounts for total student loans according to the degree pursued.

Here are a few examples:

	Starting Salary	Mid-career Salary	Maximum Student Debt
Engineering	$61,600	$101,750	$39,500
Computer Science (CS)	$56,600	$97,900	$36,500
Nursing	$52,700	$69,300	$34,000
Elementary Education	$32,400	$44,000	$21,000
Psychology	$35,000	$61,300	$22,500
Business	$41,000	$70,500	$26,500

**Exceeding these guidelines will result in lower standard of living.

** Visit www.yourpathahead.com or use the QR Code in the Appendix to see your recommended maximum student debt for more than 100 of the most common four year degrees.

A L EQ R E

Accounting is just breaking thing into pieces and adding the pieces up. If you were given a jar full of change, what would you do? Separate the quarters, dimes, nickels and pennies? And then add it all up? If so, then you can control your financial path by understanding that everything financial belongs in one of the following 5 categories:

Assets   **Liabilities**   **Equity**   **Revenue**   **Expenses**

Accounting for business and accounting for your personal financial life is the same.

A - Assets - Things worth value
> Money, buildings, vehicles, equipment, furniture

L - Liabilities - What you owe
> Bills to pay (like a power bill or phone bill), loans

EQ - Equity – Net Worth
> Assets minus liabilities

R - Revenues
> Sales, payments for services rendered

E - Expenses
> Operating costs

Everything above the line is the **Balance Sheet.** It measures where you are at a point in time. Over your life you will work to build value, and this will be measured by Equity.

Below the line is the **Income Statement**. It is the difference between revenues and expenses, or personally – what you make and what you spend. It measures how you did for a period of time, usually a year.

Here is a balance sheet, also known as a statement of net worth, for a couple at age 30 and again 20 years later:

		Kelly and Jake -at age 30	Kelly and Jake -at age 50
Assets			
	Cash and savings	$27,000	$340,000
	House	$140,000	$275,000
	Cars	$45,000	$60,000
	Personal assets	$8,000	$50,000
	Total assets	$220,000	$725,000
Liabilities			
	Car loans	$34,000	$20,000
	Mortgage on house	$115,000	$65,000
	Student loans	$36,000	$0
	Total Liabilities	$185,000	$85,000
Equity		$35,000	$640,000

When Kelly and Jake are 30, they are highly leveraged – meaning they owe a high percentage on the stuff (assets) they own. They have $35,000 in equity (net worth). The equity in their house is $25,000 ($140,000 value minus the $115,000 they owe).

At age 50, Kelly and Jake have benefited from appreciation (over time values go up, like house prices). Their total equity is now $640,000, which comes from increased income, building equity in their home, savings, and paying down other debt.

Revenues – Expenses = Net Income

In business, Net Income is sales minus the costs of operating the business. The difference is Net Income (profit). Personally, it is salary minus living expenses that determine if you are moving in a positive financial direction or negative – depending on if that difference is positive or negative. Positive means you are able to save and add to net worth (equity), and negative means you are borrowing to live and subtracts from net worth. In your twenties, especially when you are investing in your future through education, it can be typical to have years where you are spending more than you bring in. You can do your future self a favor by having a financial plan that prevents you from digging a hole your future income can't fill.

Understanding the difference between an **expense** and a **capital expenditure** is vitally important in understanding how to plan your financial path.

Capital Expenditure = Investment in the future, assets that last more than one period
> **Examples:**   House, furniture, computers, refrigerator

Capital assets generate an economic benefit or utility over time. You buy a refrigerator that lasts 20 years or furniture that will last 30. The owner of a pizza restaurant buys a pizza oven that will cook pizzas for 20 years. The owner invested in the future, and by definition the pizza oven is a capital asset. The owner of the pizza restaurant must pay employees, pay power bills, pay for cheese, dough, pepperoni, etc. Those are all operating expenses, and the sales of pizza must generate enough money to pay all the operating expenses for the restaurant to be successful and survive.

Operating Expense – Current cost of doing business
> Power bill, rent, salaries

Living expenses – Cost of living day to day
> Power bill, rent, gas, car payment (the interest), food, clothes, etc.

Here is the KEY to opening the gate to a successful financial future…

Don't turn operating expenses into long term debt

Or, said another way….

Don't borrow long term for living expenses

In your 20s, it will be necessary to leverage your income (borrow) to acquire assets. Do you want to live with your parents for 15 or 20 years so you can save enough money to buy a house? Or would you rather be able to purchase a home by borrowing from a bank? Your 20s will be your most financially challenging and demanding period of your life. Starting out on your own, you will need furniture, appliances, a car, and a place to live. Your income will not support these expenses without borrowing. That is all manageable over time and a wise use of leverage (debt). What causes the problems that lead to financial instability is borrowing for living (operating) expenses – like the power bill and gas for your car.

For 10 years, a college professor asked his classes the following questions:

"What if you go out to dinner tonight? Is that an operating expense, or an investment?"

"Operating expense," says the class.

"How about paying your cable and internet bill?"

"Operating expense," says the class.

"Putting gas in your car" says the professor.

"Operating expense," says the class.

"OK. What if you buy a house?'

This starts a discussion, and most of the class considers it an investment.

The professor adds, "What if you buy stock in Google or Apple?"

"Investment," yells the class.

"And how do we measure the value of an investment?"

"By the return," from almost everyone in the class. The class feels good and hopes these questions will be on the next test.

"All right," the professor pauses, and says "A college education? Is that an expense or an investment?"

Everyone in the class smiles. They all say "INVESTMENT", with several adding "Investment in our future!"

The professor walks around and asks "Then it is an investment in yourself, a long term asset like a contractor buying tools and equipment or a pizza restaurant owner buying a pizza oven. Is that correct?"

"Yes," exclaims the class.

"Then, how many of you calculated your return on your investment in a college education when you chose this college and your majors?"

The class is silent. In 10 years, no student has ever had an answer for that question. These students had never been asked the question. These students did not have a guide to assist them develop their path ahead when making college and career decisions.

How do you measure, or value, an investment?

Return

Return – what you make off what you put in.

$1150 Current Value
- $1000 Put in (invested)
\-
$150 Return

$150/$1,000 = 15% ROI (Return On Investment)

Calculating the return on most investments is a mathematical exercise. Calculating the Return on Education is more complex:

$$ROE_D = \frac{\uparrow \$ + \uparrow Quality\ of\ Life}{Education\ cost}$$

It is difficult to measure, in dollars, the increase in the quality of life from education. It is the combination of how much you enjoy what you do, where you live and all the other factors where your job/career affect your lifestyle.

Decide how you want to live your life and match your educational attainment to the jobs and careers that enable your chosen lifestyle.

Always consider the cost of education in relation to the future earning potential afforded by the degree. And NEVER dig a student debt hole your career can't fill.

Degrees

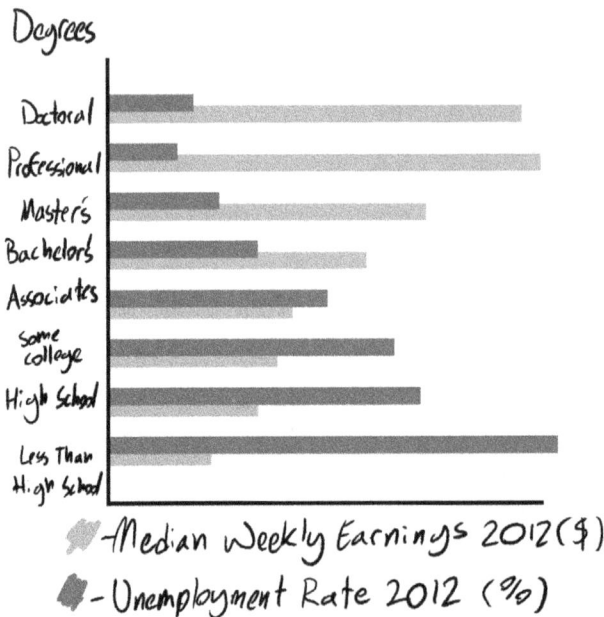

Doctoral
Professional
Master's
Bachelor's
Associates
Some college
High School
Less Than High School

- Median Weekly Earnings 2012($)
- Unemployment Rate 2012 (%)

The chart above illustrates that your options in life generally increase as you increase your level of educational attainment. This is true for the majority of people, but be aware these are averages – just like in the commonly believed statement "college graduates earn a $ 1 million more over their lifetimes than high school graduates." Nearly 35% of college graduates are underemployed – waiters, waitresses, parking lot attendants, many additional jobs that do not require a college degree. Of recent college graduates, 44% are classified as underemployed. **And the majority of those underemployed are paying student loan payments for degrees for which they are not realizing financial benefit!**

This is preventable by forming Your Path Ahead:
- Establishing goals
- Developing plans to accomplish those goals
- Calculating your ROEd (return on education)
- Not digging a student debt hole your career can't fill

Two Paths - Medicine and Construction

Luke and John finish high school the same year. John has the goal of becoming a doctor, so he enrolls in a private university with a high ranking and excellent reputation. Tuition at Private U is over $50,000/year. John receives some scholarships and other financial assistance that contributes about a third of the cost, so he takes out student loans for $35,000 each year. John can't work while in college because the demands of the science classes require that he spends 60 to 70 hours per week focused on his schoolwork to attain the excellent grades necessary for admission to medical school. John ends his undergraduate career with $155,000 in student loans (what he borrowed and accrued interest).

John is accepted and goes to medical school, where he borrows an additional $142,000 although his family still supports him with living expenses. He graduates, and now his student loan debt totals $318,000 (with accrued interest).

After medical school, doctors must complete an average of eight years of residency and the other requirements necessary to become board certified in their specialization. Physicians earn around $40,000/year while in residency, so John barely makes enough to support himself while he works 70 and 80 hour weeks. He delays the repayment of his student loans until he is certified.

On John's 35th birthday he receives his certification in General Surgery. He has been in "school" for 31 years, and for the first time in his life he will make more money than he spends. His net worth is negative $300,000. His student loan debt is $360,000, and he must start repayment of $4,143/month for the next 10 years. If he attains the average salary in general surgery, he will make $265,000/year, and his take home pay will be around $15,000/month. After paying his student loan payment, and putting a significant contribution to his retirement account (because he has not worked very much he has very little in retirement) he will realize less than $8,000/month. If he pays his payment on time, he will be 45 years old when he has paid off his education.

THEN

NOW*

HOT ROD

*NOTE: Drop in standard of living not to scale

Over the last 15 years many doctors have seen declines in their average incomes due to all the pressures on health care in the United States, such as insurance, government regulation, etc. This lower income, combined with the explosion in tuition for both undergraduate and medical school (an average of $275,000 for private medical school and $200,000 for public) has resulted in lower financial rewards in the field of medicine.

Luke went to work in construction after high school. He learned on the job, and by the time he was 25, he was supervising a crew. People he knew, and didn't know, were constantly contacting him to ask if he could come to their house and work. He began doing jobs on the weekend like building decks, remodeling rooms and more. He was also financially stable and bought a house. He built a reputation for good work and was constantly turning down extra work. Understanding the opportunity, he quit his job and started his own construction/remodeling company. By age 30 he was making $80,000 a year and had student loan debt of zero. He sold his first house for a gain and bought one bigger. When Luke turned 35 he was making $125,000/year with a net worth over $300,000, which included over $100,000 in retirement savings.

Luke has a 16 year advantage over John in earnings before they turn 35. Even then, John has another 10 years of constraints paying off school loans. They will both be past the age of 55 before John is able to surpass Luke in accumulated wealth (net worth).

You don't have to be Luke, or John. And there are many careers in between. The key is to find YOUR balance between lifestyle and money.

Chapter 6

The Path to Knowledge

It's not the ...   It's the ...

bat   batter

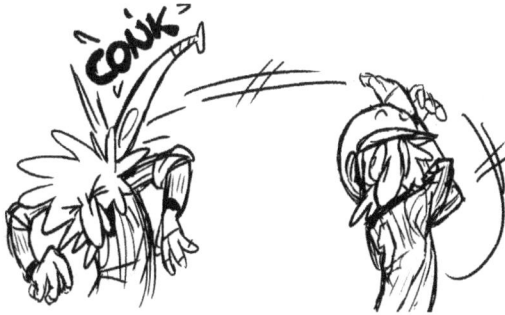

It's not the ...   It's the ...

arrow   archer

It's not the ...   It's the ...

school   student

It's not the …   It's the …

DEGREE   ABILITY TO APPLY KNOWLEDGE

In the future it will be:

It's not the …   It's the …

Credentials   Ability to produce

The processes of MEASUREMENT, VALUATION and PERSPEC-TIVE (MVP) will change. The possession of a credential (usually a degree) is no longer satisfactory proof of ability. Employers will focus on production – what employees can do – not what a piece of paper says the person has done. Many factors have combined to reduce credentials as proof of ability, skill and knowledge:

- Dramatic growth and proliferation of online degrees. Many online universities have been labeled as "degree factories" that were only focused on revenue and not student learning. In other words they were selling credentials while recommending that the students borrow the money for these degrees.

- "Traditional" colleges and universities loosened standards to compete with the for-profit and other online degree programs. Also, with greater percentages of high school graduates entering college, the average college student is now less prepared than in previous generations.

- With more than 50% of students entering college never graduating, colleges have pressures to focus on "student success." The results are "grade inflation" (making classwork easier) and directing students into easier, non-challenging programs of study.

Putting MEASUREMENT and VALUATION into PERSPECTIVE concerning college degrees, it is simply the ADDED VALUE one receives from the degree. Colleges and universities have no criteria to measure or define the value added from their programs.

The bottom line is simple. It is the individual student that holds the key to unlocking value in education.

- Know your ROEd

- Set goals and develop your plan

- Match your return from education to your future income, lifestyle, and maximum debt

- 80% of 10th graders plan to attend college

- 30% of college students drop out before their second year

- 50% of college students do not graduate

- 85% of college students move back home after graduating

- Tuition per year:
  - Community College - $4,500
  - In-state Public - $17,500
  - Private - $35,500

- A college degree is worth approximately $250,000 more over a lifetime for 80% of college graduates (removing the top 20% of earners)

- SHOES will provide your traction in your path ahead

  - Strategy – goals and plans
  - Holes – don't dig holes like too much debt
  - Options – create, explore
  - Experience – can't be taught – gain it – all work is good
  - Skills – develop and learn to learn

- 20% of working America is underemployed

- 15 years is the average time it takes to pay off a student loan

- Baby Boomers will be retiring. It is a large generation, and there will be jobs for those that have prepared themselves with skills and knowledge

- College students average 27 hours a week on academics because too many want classes that are easy just to get a degree. Doing this can turn four fun years into 60 years of financial struggles.

- Learning is 5% hearing, 10% watching, and 85% doing.

- Every time a student "cuts" or "skips" a class, they are throwing away between $60 and $110. Do you pay for dinner and not eat?

- Studies indicate, on average, every class skipped lowers the student's final grade three points

- Determine your own time management:

	URGENT	NOT URGENT
IMPORTANT	·FIRES ·TORNADOES	·EXERCISE · JOB
NOT IMPORTANT	·DISTRACTIONS ·PHONE CALLS	·TV SHOWS ·PHONE GAMES

- 40% of college students attend part-time.

- 71% of college students work. Of those, 20% work more than 35 hours

- 50% of non-full time working students work 20+ hours per week

- Working students too often prioritize their jobs over their education. If you must work, consider taking less hours in school so that you have the appropriate time to perform your schoolwork well.

- Don't settle for an "easier" major because of time. Just take more time to finish school.

- Your first JOB starts the day you graduate high school.
  o   Approach learning after high school as a job and start with the end in mind.
  o   Know your ROEd. Think of the return when selecting colleges and programs of study
  o   Take GAP years. If you don't like school and don't know why you are there, don't dig a bigger hole. Get a job. Volunteer. Get active and get experience. Pursue your education when you are ready.

- Over 75% of college students are "non-traditional" (commuters, family, employed, older) meaning less than a quarter of college students attend at a full time residential campus

- Excess credits are classes that don't count toward your degree. Changing majors and transferring between colleges accounts for most excess credits. Most graduates of two-year and four-year institutions have nearly one year of credits that cannot be applied to their degrees. These cost time and money. Set goals and plan in order to keep these to a minimum.

- There will be a shortfall of 15 million college educated individuals in 10 years. You are now in the Knowledge Economy, the Information Age. Prepare.

- Success is when preparation meets opportunity.

- Problems are opportunities. Those that solve problems will be successful.

What is the real value of a college education?

It is the increase of knowledge and skills added during the educational process that can be applied for productive lives and careers.

How can this be measured? It can't be measured precisely and accurately. Can success be measured just in dollars – such as salaries of the graduates? Or happiness? Is there a definitive happiness scale? Because of the absence of any true measure that puts an accurate value of the difference between degrees between different colleges, systems have been devised to rank colleges utilizing the following criteria:

- Undergraduate academic reputation
  - o   Polls of administrators of other colleges

- Student selectivity
  - o   SAT, ACT and high school grades
  - o   The more selective the school, the higher the ranking

- Faculty resources
  - o   Average class size, faculty compensation, percentage of full-time vs. part-time faculty, and percentage faculty with terminal degrees (highest degree in field)

- Graduation and retention rates

- Financial resources
  - o   Spending per student in relation to all other factors

- Alumni giving

These rankings are for the colleges and universities as a whole. Within each university or college exists strengths and weaknesses. A university may have an excellent program in sports management or mathematics and weaker programs in psychology or business administration. Or the opposite may be true.

These ranking criteria are inexact. The most weight is on reputation –
as valued by administrators at other colleges. The second biggest factor is the
abilities of the students they accept. Students who had high grades and high
SAT and ACT scores generally continue to perform exceptionally well in
college.

Selection of a college or university should not be on someone else's
ranking or what a friend said. It should be based on how it fits into your
path ahead, your goals, and your plans.

This guidebook is designed to inform and expose you to the following
concepts:
- Why economic, educational, and population issues will affect your future
- When you are living within the context of change over the history of human advancement
- How to set goals and plan for your future
- Where your money will go
- Who controls your financial future and lifestyle (You)
- What choices and options are available to you

Understand these concepts, and think about your future.

The final story...

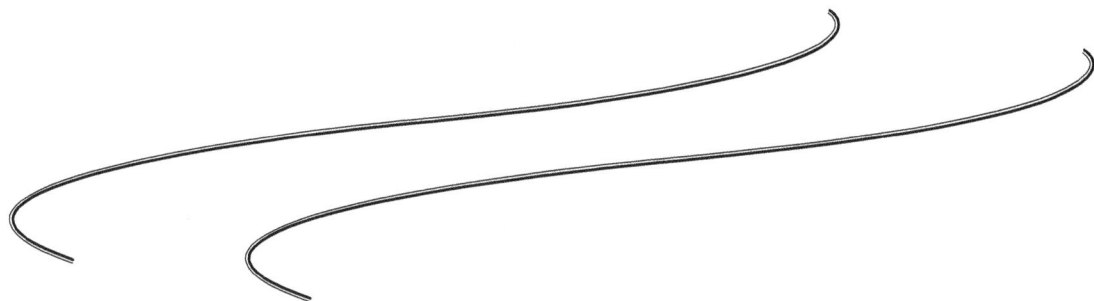

...is yours.

Summary of The Path to Knowledge

- It's not the bat that hits home runs, it's the batter. It will not be the school that makes your career; it will be your choices that define your path.

- In the future your ability to be productive will be more important than credentials.

- Beware of using college rankings as a deciding factor in school choice. The rankings are for the whole institution, and not by programs. There are rankings available by programs.

- Learning is 5% hearing, 10% watching, and 85% doing.

- Colleges and universities can teach you a lot, but they cannot teach EXPERIENCE. Experience comes from your output.

- Don't settle for "easier" degrees because of part-time work. If you must work a significant amount of time, take fewer classes each semester. Remain focused on your long term goals.

- What is a few years compared to 50? Your careers should last around fifty years. Take time off from school if undecided, but work and gain experience.

- Problems are opportunities.

- Success is when preparation meets opportunity. Your goal in acquiring knowledge and skills is to be prepared for your opportunities in life.

Appendix

Use the QR Code below to go to <u>yourpathahead.com</u>

Glossary

Advanced Placement (AP) – A program administered by the College Board through which a student can earn college credit for examinations taken while in high school.

Capital Expense - are expenses that create future benefits. They are investment in the future; i.e. House, Furniture, Computer, etc…

College-Level Examination Program (CLEP) – Examinations in under graduate college courses that present the opportunity to show college-level achievement. The exams are administered at UAF Testing Services online to provide immediate score results.

Consumer Price Index (CPI) - measures changes in the price level of a market basket of consumer goods and services purchased by households. The CPI in the United States is defined by the Bureau of Labor Statistics as "a measure of the average change over time in the prices paid by urban consumers for a market basket of consumer goods and services."

Debt Ratio - the ratio of total liabilities of a business to its total assets, ranging from 0.00 to 1.00. A higher value indicates that a larger portion of company's assets are claimed by creditors, which means it will be more difficult to obtain loans. Debt ratio of 0.5 means that half of an entity's assets are financed through debts.

Double-Half – Output must be two times input; Input must equal half of output, where output equals productivity and input equals money in pocket; your output (work) doubles your input (pay) and during your career, that gap will most likely get wider.

Expected Family Contribution (EFC) – The amount of a family's resources (income and assets) that the federal financial aid formula considers available to help pay for school.

<u>Financial Need</u> - The difference between the cost of education (student budget) and Expected Family Contribution (EFC)

<u>Flip Generation</u> - The history of mankind over time can be measured in terms of the rate of change and the acceleration of change in respect to the effects on advancements in quality of life. This rate of change is quantified using "same" and "different" as the variables – in effect indicating the change in how people live their lives between generations. The Flip Generation – people born between 1997 and 2016 –are the first generation where things affecting their lives are more different than the same.

<u>Flip Day</u> – Add 6 months to your birthdate – this is your Flip Day. On this day each year reevaluate your 5 year goals and progress. Go to our website – yourpathahead.com – to save your goals each year on your Flip Day.

<u>Happiness Equation</u>– (Happiness is a function of the various components of life over time) a formula for life; a platform for combining the financial aspects and the components that add up for quality of life; i.e. the trade off between making money and doing what you love and how you live.

<u>Living Expenses</u> – cost of living day to day including power, rent, gas, food, etc…

<u>Operating Expense</u> – ongoing expenses that insure continued operation including maintenance and monthly bills; current cost of doing business including power, bills, rent, and salaries.

<u>Productivity</u> - the quality, state, ability or fact of being able to generate, create, enhance, or bring forth goods, services, or profits

<u>ROED</u> – Return on Education, added value an education brings after investment.

Stafford Loan – Federally guaranteed, low interest loan for students. Two Types: Subsidized (need-based) and unsubsidized (non-need based). Both types defer payments until a student leaves school, however the government pays the interest on a subsidized load while the student is in school, whereas the unsubsidized loans collect interest when the loan is funded with payments being deferred until principle payments begin (typically 6 months after program completion or student is no longer at least half time enrolled).

Transfer Credit – Refers to units (hours) of academic credit awarded at a receiving institution in recognition of college level credit earned at another institution. Operating under a variety of systems (Semester vs. Quarter), hour credit may be converted to quarter hour credit by multiplying 1.5. The receiving institute does not typically award transfer credit to credits received by other institutes if they do not comply with the receiving institutes catalog, course description or program.

Zero Sum Game - A give and take balance of life. If one gains, the other loses and vice versa. Example: Four students buy one pizza. If one student eats more than ¼ of pizza, another student has to eat less. If you want more money, you have to give up time, etc.

Solutions

The following are solutions to the problems on pages 55-57

1)	$7.50
2)	$8.50
3)	$1,920
4)	3
5)	1 Hour 51 Minutes
6)	15 Minutes
7)	43
8)	$110
9)	9
10)	Thursday
11)	60%
12)	40

*For full solutions see yourpathahead.com

Useful Websites for College Information

- College Board
  collegeboard.org

- National Center for Education Statistics – College Navigator
  nces.ed.gov/collegenavigator

- Your Path Ahead – Maximum Student Loan Debt Guidelines
  yourpathahead.com/studentloancalc.php

www.ingramcontent.com/pod-product-compliance
Lightning Source LLC
Chambersburg PA
CBHW081011040426
42443CB00016B/3488